NOTE TO PARENTS

This well known fairytale has been specially written and adapted for 'first readers', that is, for children who are just beginning to read by themselves. However, for those not yet able to read, then why not read this story aloud to your child, pointing to the words and talking about the pictures? There is a word list at the back of the book which identifies difficult words and explains their meaning in the context of the story.

Aladdin

retold by Clare Humphreys
illustrated by Gill Guile

Copyright © MCMLXXXVIII by World International Publishing Limited.
All rights reserved.
Published in Great Britain by World International Publishing Limited.
An Egmont Company, Egmont House,
P.O. Box 111, Great Ducie Street,
Manchester M60 3BL.
Printed in Italy.
ISBN 7235 8888 0

Long ago there was a little boy
called Aladdin.
One day a man said to him,
"I am your long lost uncle.
Tell your mother
I shall visit her tomorrow."

Aladdin's uncle came with presents.
He said he had been away
for a long time.
But this was not true.
He was not Aladdin's uncle at all.
He was a wicked magician!

But he was so kind
that Aladdin's mother believed him.

One day the magician took Aladdin
to the hills.
They stopped at a big rock.
When the magician spoke,
it rolled aside.

There was a cave!
"In the cave is a lamp," said
the magician. "Bring it to me."
He gave Aladdin a ring.
"This will keep you safe,"
he said.

Aladdin went into the cave.
He saw lots of gold.
"Get the lamp!"
shouted the magician.

Aladdin picked up some gold.
Then he picked up the lamp.
"Give me the lamp!"
called the magician.
"Not until I am out of here,"
replied Aladdin.

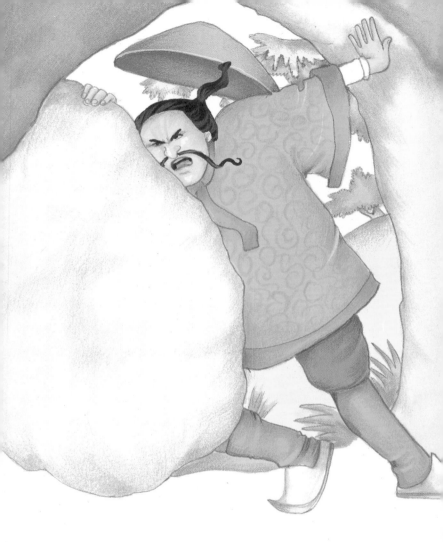

This made the magician very angry.
He rolled the rock back
across the cave opening.
Aladdin was trapped!

Aladdin began to cry.
But as he wiped the tears away,
he rubbed the magician's ring.
And a genie appeared!

"I am the genie of the ring.
I will help you," said the genie.
"Please take me home,"
said Aladdin.
And in an instant
he was back at home.

He told his mother about the cave.
Then he gave her the lamp.
When she rubbed it
another genie appeared!

"I am the genie of the lamp.
I will help you," he said.
"Bring us food," said Aladdin.
The genie disappeared.
A moment later he came back.
In his hands was a huge plate of food!

The genie gave Aladdin and
his mother all they wanted.
Soon they had lovely clothes
and a fine house.

One day Aladdin saw
the Emperor's daughter.
She was beautiful.
He fell in love with her at once.
Aladdin made his mind up
to marry the princess.

The Emperor said that
Aladdin could marry his daughter.
The princess liked Aladdin
very much too.
Soon they were married.
They went to live in a fine palace
that the genie built for them.

Then the wicked magician heard
about Aladdin's good luck.
He knew that
Aladdin must have the lamp!
So he thought up a plan
to get the lamp for himself.

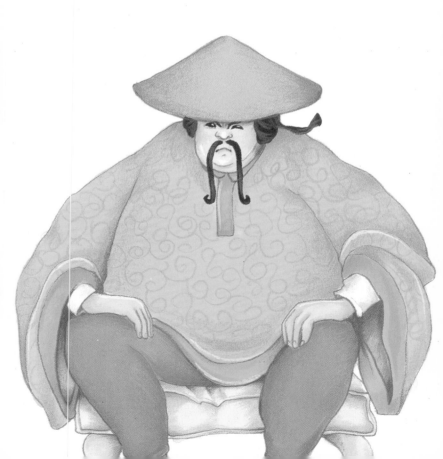

He went to the palace
dressed like a pedlar.
He had a basket of shiny lamps.
"New lamps for old lamps,"
he called.
The princess gave him
Aladdin's lamp.
She did not know it was special.

The magician rubbed the lamp hard.
And the genie appeared in a flash.
"Take the princess and myself
far away," said the magician.

The Emperor found out
his daughter had gone.
He sent for Aladdin.
"You have three days to
find her," the Emperor said.
"Or I will cut off your head!"

Aladdin thought of
the genie of the ring.
He asked the genie for help.
The genie said he would take him
to the princess.

The princess was so happy
to see Aladdin.
Then he told her about his plan.
"Invite the magician to dinner.
I will do the rest," he said.

Aladdin put some sleeping powder
in the magician's wine.
It sent him straight to sleep.
Then Aladdin took the lamp
from the magician's belt.
In a flash, the genie
took them all back home.

The Emperor was so pleased
to see his daughter again.
Aladdin told him everything.
And the wicked magician
was put in jail!

Aladdin hid the ring and the lamp
in a secret room.
No one could make mischief
with them again.
In time, Aladdin became
the new Emperor.
He was a very kind Emperor.
His people grew to love him
and the princess.

New words

Did you see a lot of new words in the story? Here is a list of some hard words from the story, and what they mean.

appeared
the very first time you saw the genie

arrived
when the magician came to Aladdin's house

believed
Aladdin's mother thought the magician was telling the truth

disappeared
when the genie went away

Emperor
an emperor is like a king

genie
someone who makes wishes true